AF390575

If I Only Knew Corinthians 13

Love that failed to prosper: A book of ocean deep, raw, and broken-hearted poetry

Amber Feliciano

Copyright © Amber Feliciano
All Rights Reserved.

This book has been self-published with all reasonable efforts taken to make the material error-free by the author. No part of this book shall be used, reproduced in any manner whatsoever without written permission from the author, except in the case of brief quotations embodied in critical articles and reviews.

The Author of this book is solely responsible and liable for its content including but not limited to the views, representations, descriptions, statements, information, opinions, and references ["Content"]. The Content of this book shall not constitute or be construed or deemed to reflect the opinion or expression of the Publisher or Editor. Neither the Publisher nor Editor endorse or approve the Content of this book or guarantee the reliability, accuracy, or completeness of the Content published herein and do not make any representations or warranties of any kind, express or implied, including but not limited to the implied warranties of merchantability, fitness for a particular purpose.

The Publisher and Editor shall not be liable whatsoever...

Made with ❤ on the BookLeaf Publishing Platform
www.bookleafpub.in
www.bookleafpub.com

Dedication

You have watched my every dream fall onto the ground;
Witnessed me unsew myself in despair.
You have always admired,
And have always been proud
When I decide to put glitter on and stitch myself
together again.
You are the bookend that keeps me stable;
I think of myself as a balloon that you hold tightly in
your hand.
You are the logic
And I am the dream—
Together, we make a perfect team.
To my Omma, who has always believed in me—
My perfect, perfect beauty.

Preface

"Weeping may endure for a night, but joy cometh in the morning." — Psalms 30:5

Though the night,
The night
Can leave us mourning.

To experience the light
Is worth enduring.

If you believe in love,
You believe in God.

Acknowledgements

Thank you.

To the Holy Trinity — I am speechless.

My wife, Jessica Robyn Feliciano, for always believing, enduring, and never losing hope.

My deceased father — the story and happy ending are determined through me so your passing doesn't go in vain.

My Omma — thank you.

Mallory Elizabeth Godwin, you are undeniably turbulent in love, and I stare at you in awe.

My ex-fiancé — who taught me what love was not.

My former Jewish lover — a confused man who inspired me to live and die for my beliefs; how pitiful and desperate it is to try to make someone love you.

Lauren Parker — I blankly stare as I think of you.

And to Tango, my sweet, precious boy.

It's Forbidden

My Endangered Species
Oh, how you hold my hand;
Squeeze it until it breaks,
With your strength.
But wrap my neck, for it is forbidden
And of bad taste.
I'll do anything for your survival,
As long as you let me live
Or die
In your arms.
I wouldn't want to be anyone else's prey,
My sweetest predator.

Natural Disaters

I'd wait for you through the blizzard,
Through the hurricane,
Through the forest fires,
And scorching hot days.
I'll draw your name
In the sand;
On the beach
At a far distance from the ocean.
And I will know you're waiting for me too,
Yet a tsunami hits and violently destroys you and me.

Strawberry

I once wondered,
Is her hair strawberry,
Or do her kisses reach your soul?
Does her head touch your shoulder?
Does she have the glitter?
Does she have the gold?
And through all of my fantasies,
About her eyes and about her stare,
I realized they may all be true.
She may be perfect, but
All she has is you.

Short Hair

I met you with short hair,
Wanting to flee toward Mexico—
Blue eyes and blonde hair.
I bloomed just for you,
The way a flower salutes the sun.
Little did I know you would tear my heart.
I met you with nothing but my love to spare.
There were glasses of Henny by the pool;
And we shared
Our fallen dreams that never came true.
I was the glitter,
You were the glue—
Now I'm stuck on you.
While you gather your dreams
That you thought would never come true,
Trying to make them into something with someone new.

Monitor

I put my ear to your chest,
And hear your heartbeat
Until my heart beats at the same time.
We are on a life monitor that is synchronized.
I put my ear to your chest,
And hear the beats fading,
And my heart fades too.
I put my ear to your chest,
I hear your heart whisper nothing
As my monitor starts beeping.

Trash

What if I steal your art,
Carry you around to my destinations,
Searching for my other half?
Wandering the Earth with your art,
I would never be alone.
Until the time they come along,
I'd carry part of a piece you'd drawn
By your tender hands—
Hands that touched my body,
Hands that reached my soul,
Hands that took my breath away.
The day I met them,
My true soulmate,
I immediately threw your art away,
The way you threw me away.

Wood

Wonder if I met you
At a different time,
During a different spring.
Jesus is where he left you,
Somewhere you thought he'd forget,
Somewhere you thought he couldn't see.
And I never imagined I'd fret you,
For your perfect figure is dissipating,
And everything is obscured—
I can't see a thing.
Where is your mind escaping?
When I'm catching you awake in the night,
With the light on,
But you're not saying a word.
Would your heart hate me
If I packed my belongings
Without a smirk?
Would you blame me?
Because it's something you do
When you're stubborn,

When you're blue.
The heart is fickle.
I tend to wander,
Not knowing who I belong to.
But I thought my love was true;
I thought it was for you.
For leaves that are committed to a tree
Fall too.
Autumn is near—
Lighter fluid, lighter, and wood are all we would need.
We can start a fire,
And we can burn our hearts together gently,
Mending them into one;
Curing the illness of separation.
We'll make ourselves belong together,
Even if we might hate it.

Zilker Park

You are the sunlight peeking through the trees
When I sit in Zilker Park,
Pondering your memories.
You are the purple and green hues in the mosaic
That I'd gather as a child—
Helen Keller's *light in the darkness,*
The fear and turmoil that happens in the night.
The overlooked boundaries of the sea,
The bikers embarking on cliffs,
Mountains yet to be explored—
Territories that don't belong on Earth.
I am the sadness in a pit,
Daunted with big eyes and a pout to kiss.
While I look in the rearview mirror,
Fighting for my life,
The controversy of being split into two,
Understanding nothing at all
Except that I loved more than anyone I ever knew.

Disgusting Feet

I can't say you come
And do it to me anymore.
It's your beauty that allures me,
But your feet are of many burdens.
One foot is bare, half inside my French doors,
The other foot barely tucked in a shoe,
And your hand is holding the matching pair,
So when you flee, you can run away—
Your feet, full of mud.
You run back and take one shoe off again,
And I invite you to take a step inside my French door.
You fill my home with the filth of your footprint,
Then you leave again—one foot out of the door.
I don't care anymore
Who taught you to run,
What your childhood was like,
Where you learned from.
I care about myself
And you dirtying my floors—
The pain it brings

To have to clean up my home.
Please, stay outside.
I'll lock my doors,
But it's not necessary.
You'll never try to forcefully come inside my house
Because you don't want to come inside.
It's cold, and your feet need warmth.
But when you knock
And I let you in,
You invade my space,
And I despise feet.
So, instead of asking you to leave me alone,
I'll let you knock once,
Not open the door,
And you'll leave.
That'll be the end
Of you and me—
I will no longer let you rambunctiously explore my
indoors,
And I will no longer have to clean the tile marked with
your disgraceful feet.

Cherry Red Dress

We were in the kitchen,
The chimney was steaming.
You were making lobster with butter,
As you did every weekend.
I choked on my food that night;
My throat was clogged,
And you knew exactly what to do to save me.
You were so proud
To have saved me.
I cried and cried as I stared at the room blankly.
My mom was grateful for you to have saved me.
Do you understand, as I do,
How many times you have saved me?
We were in a mobile home,
Stopping through the park
From out of town,
And I saw something different in your eyes—
Your pupils were big,
You squinted so small.
My sweet father,

You said that you had stopped,
But I knew you did not.
My boyfriend at the time saved me;
He knew exactly what was going on
As I tried to battle your addiction.
I think he knew it was the last time
I would see what soon would be missing.
I was in San Francisco not too long after;
I bought you a one-way ticket.
You carried yourself on a train
To be with my mom
And stayed with her as you recovered.
I deleted our texts;
I would find myself reading them in your voice
And I would miss you beyond words.
But you would quote things by Helen Keller:
"God is in me as the sun is in the color and fragrance of a
flower...
The light in my darkness, the voice in my silence."
And I would pause for a second—
Just a second—
While I gasped for you in my despair.
My mom found you
After a long night
Of you telling her jokes.
She cried at your humor;
Laughter filled the home.

I felt it in California.
But there was a contrast that night
Of the darkness of forgiveness.
You lost to your disease.
I flew after choking nights
Back home
To see you.
I laid my body on yours,
With my cherry dress
And luxury perfume.
And seeing your cold, breathless face
Changed me in a way I'd never find home again.
My psychiatrist has saved me ever since
With tiny little pills
To cure my pretty little mind.
But I still remember my cherry red dress
And my perfumed scent.
I never wore these pieces again;
They are all too desinence.

No Umbrella

The light dangled with a string
That could faint with the wind.
Oh, how you left so cheaply,
With a heavyweight—
Now you're a whisper in my head.
Am I distant in fever?
Are you the shadow that lingers in my bed?
Oh, Father,
Am I prettier now that you've left?
Are my clothes bejeweled in amber,
Made for a woman who was once a little girl?
Questions of the unknown
Lead me to shame—
My heart built of straws and bones.
Now I'm grown,
And I walked into the rain
With nothing to cover my head.
As I do, I do,
And I knew, from unfamiliar faces,
I could find you.

I was in a circus, but far from a clown—
Lost in a child's mind,
Sick and unwell.
You took my hand and kissed up to my neck,
Asking if we could get married,
As if we wouldn't see each other again.
A coward you were for never asking once more
When I was a scared young lady and you were now fully
grown.
I'd see the first time I saw you,
And I loved you—I did.
When I'd wear my brown heels,
My height made you question what it was to be a man.
And I'm not mad at you, or you,
Or him, or them.
I'm a piece of wood lit by the heat of my hands
For a broken world that spins on a crooked hex.
You both left me,
And I'd rather be happy as if we all never met.

Ink Drips, Ink Falls, Ink Draws

I witnessed a story
Of a beautiful young woman who went to my school.
I knew two of her sisters personally,
Attached at the foot.
Suddenly, the oldest passed in her sleep,
With no cause.
Rest in peace.
Heaven was ready to take her.
She was in her 20s.
She had a baby.
He would gaze at the picture in a frame and smile.
When he didn't have a mom anymore,
He would look at her for hours.
I could see every memory of her life
Playing like a brightly covered, joyful film.
Yet, I only knew her at a distance.
Ink was filled.
A story that would continue to be written,
Feathered,

Losing color often,
Dripping like a black pen touching white sheets.
Her mom would share her writings about her faith and
God.
She couldn't wait to be in His kingdom.
She believed she had a mission.
She believed she'd see those she loved.
She believed in Jesus.
She believed in Heaven, that there was a cause.
I believe her too—
Both of her sisters snorted and needled their arms
When their sister was put in a tube.
Heroin and fentanyl—
Soul-sucking tools.
The more you love someone, the more you grieve.
They all loved her unconditionally.
Afterward, the middle sister passed away.
She was sober and rehabilitated—
One little mishap,
One little time she was bent out of shape
Over a disgusting, drug-loving,
Soul-crushing,
Demon-hunting fault.
Pieces of sand,
All alone,
Turning into a deformed glass—
Empty and unused.

The ink drips,
The ink falls,
The ink draws.
Two daughters covered in dirty earth grass—
Gut-wrenching and somber,
The unseen latch to souls,
Despicable goons.
Burn them to the pits of hell.
My God,
Burn it all to the ground
And love us, you're human,
Little fools.

If I Only Knew Corinthians 13

If only I knew what love looked like,
I wouldn't have wasted my time
Incanting on your images.
If I only knew what love looked like,
I wouldn't have asked for the cards
To see what you were thinking.
If I only knew what love looked like,
I wouldn't have thrown flowers on the floor,
Screaming in pain about how the broken glass hurt.
If I only knew what love looked like,
I wouldn't have torn you into threads with my words.
I wouldn't have argued,
I wouldn't have sworn.
If I only knew what love looked like,
I may have enjoyed my twenties,
Instead of grieving in bar bathroom stalls.
If I only knew what love looked like,
I would have read Corinthians 13
And gasped at the mercy for breath.

Describing love in supernatural ways
As they love in Heaven.
If I only knew Corinthians 13,
It could have saved the love that did not prosper.

Grapefruit

I once made you cry in the shower,
So loud, screeching in my ears
As if it were a plea for life.
All the hurtful things I said,
My tongue filled with spite.
I never bring up your wrongdoings
Because I now know how to love.
However, we are different in many ways—
So different that I cry the same way
And in the same setting, I hurt you that day.
It took many years to forgive myself
For my entitlement,
For being venomous, as I thought
You were the cause of my pain.
As an adolescent, I faced many turmoils.
What we thought of as love,
What we thought was the truth—
I blamed you.
Now, we're older, and I see my beautiful face age,
And I look like you.

You've moved on to the next page;
I should too.
And I admire you, for I have created
Disasters far worse,
And you supported me through the hurt.
I understand how our story shaped us,
In a way, you needed me to keep you safe.
And now, you speedily race
To help me the same.
We were in a tragic story together,
Now survivors, and we needed each other.
I am so glad that you birthed me,
Even on days when I am ready
To dispose of my body
And fall into a groundbreaking earthquake.
Only you can understand what we went through,
From the times we hopped fences to run away.
Once, we lived in a car for one night and one day.
You are the only one who knows me
And the danger we faced—
Finding needles and burnt spoons covering the floor
To the point we were afraid.
So we put hard-covered shoes and gloves on
So they would not penetrate.
But, wow, you were my joy,
You were my saving grace.
I'd wake up every day and kiss your face.

After Dad passed away, our hearts physically hurt.
We would stop, put our hands to our chests
While tears would burst.
All of our hopes and dreams we thought were
guaranteed
Quickly withered, permanently.
For many weeks, I could not speak;
For many months, my body was covered with a
bedsheet.
I don't think we'll ever be the same.
Our eyes have even changed.
But you always tell me that this is life—
It is nuanced and bittersweet,
Like a grapefruit.
And I reply, I am too weak
To taste such an awful thing.

Greedy Man

I now understand
How man
Can take all the land.
If it's anything like my love for you,
I am greedy enough
To take all of it too.

Shame

I remember you during what I thought was a better day,
Long blonde hair and beautiful big eyes that stared my
way.
I think about you when the morning rains,
Sun showers and the shameful feelings of pain.
When you looked at me, I felt the rays of light
Hitting my hair, turning it from dark brown to light red.
It's never been the same,
And I have to hold onto these memories,
To hold onto you.
Because of the thought that you'd be here for not much
longer,
Leaving my heart oozing with blood until I'm purple and
blue.
If morning came, I'd turn to see your gorgeous face;
I would slowly burn to the ground if it were empty.
But I'll always run away before it could ever end;
I cannot bear to see another breathless face,
Another addiction that leaves you with just skin attached
to your bones,

Because you refuse to let your tastebuds explore love.
Imagine the shattering of my world when he left me—
Except it's you, and I can't be sewn back together,
Only stitched like a flapping doll.
People play in a mental room—

M. Godwin

I elongated my limbs,
So elegant and free,
As the ocean piano played on my body.
Where had I been when you needed me?
Walking the sands by the beach.
Where had I been when you cried to me?
My feet were in grains as I pondered the love you give
unconditionally.
Broken we all are,
As I smelled the sea—
Broken like an earthquake causing a tsunami.
And the breeze parted my eyes;
You have such a good heart with many goodbyes—
Not impacting because it was never the end;
It was only a new beginning,
My best friend.
And I questioned,
Where was I when darkness covered all of the light?
I was pondering how shattering it is to be alive.
But with you, my eyes laugh

As the moon moves the tide.
A blessing you are, for your kindness and boldness,
Make me not want to hide.
So, where were you when I ran on the shoreline?
I found you hopeless
And held you as you cried—
And I do it for you gladly, time after time.

Sparkle

I imploded when I saw her face;
I knew she would be the art of my story.
She became my world,
The parts I was missing.
She could do no wrong,
No harm—
All that is perfect in the world.
And I'd shield her from anything that would take her
innocence away.
Naively, she walked,
With her honey eyes at a distance,
Glitter on her face.
She trusted me, and I broke it in innocent ways.
On my shoulders, I held her
As a wave would crash,
As a wave would fall.
And I promised her I would not let her go,
Until we fell under the current,
Knocked down and yielded to the ground.
Yet something so simple

Broke her inside;
For I made a promise that meant so much in her world.
We laughed, but I could see she wanted to cry.
I promised her many things,
Though I let her down.
We experienced monumental moments
That a camera could not capture.
I was starstruck by every molecule of her being;
Everything she touched turned to sparkle—
Because that is who she is!
When my mind would flash back to torment,
Her presence accepted me for all I had been.
It was as though she tore every bone in my chest
To rip out my heart,
Just to hear it beating in her hands.
I could let immaturity fill my mouth
And easily claim she took my unconditional love for
granted,
But I'd rather express that it was worth my years,
And I'd do it foolishly again, like metal attracts a
magnet.
Two fragile girls who needed each other
Like stars need the night
Would silently say goodbye.
Hush, hush, hush,
I'm not mad at you;
Don't let that thought stop you from living your life.

Tango

Powerful sunsets after the rain;
I think of you.
How you liked to eat,
How you would steal my food,
Begging for a bone or a treat.
I loved our walks together,
You thoughtfully smelling the air.
You weren't even mine,
But I cherished your presence;
You were a true companion.
No barks at the mailman—
Only joy when you saw your dad.
You touched me like no other.
My sweet Tango,
You were my secret best friend.

Satin Sheets

I've had the experience of love,
Such as it would have been in the 1960s.
The door opens to a Cadillac,
Flowers waiting to be received.
Menus with hidden prices,
Casual and repeated.
I've had the experience of love—
Visiting museums,
Modeling,
Shopping sprees,
Yachting,
And the Beverly Hills Plaza with a balcony jacuzzi.
I've had the experience of love
That swallowed me whole
And spat me out in pieces.
I had the experience of love
Where we wrote letters and emails,
And I would leave my lips to sign it.
Looking foolish,
I would cry, I would plead,

I would beg to be held and loved—
Silly me.
However,
I hear experiences of love
That involve phone calls and no calls.
I hear they take you out to dinner
And have a fantastic time in their bed,
But they never text or call again.
Or they think you owe them intimacy
Because they bought you a happy hour drink,
Expecting payment for their facade money.
You want someone who surprises you
With glamour and chardonnay,
Love that doesn't dissipate.
I don't care about material things,
But it's sensational to wrap yourself
In satin sheets for a heartbreak that's guaranteed.
If it were me, I would do it for you.
If it is you, do it for me.
But if they ever leave your text unread,
I highly suggest not to plead,
Not to beg.
Cry gently,
And never let a fool break your heart again.

Destiny in the Sky

Electric waves crash
Inside my stomach,
And I thought I felt you—
But it was just a shock
From unbearable news.
The burdens you took
From all the beatings I endured,
From the eyes that turned black,
That turned blue.
A baby that will never speak,
A dream that I once had, now unfulfilled.
And I wanted you,
But I'm not good enough
To love someone so pure and new.
Every contraction, wanting to bleed,
To feel what it's like to give life to you.
I'm sorry.
I'll still feel your essence in my womb,
And I'll keep it there until my death—
Without a touch,

Without a scent,
Without our existence,
Like Destiny in the Sky.
Love that failed to prosper
Like so many others.
Yet, I believe—
There will always be a tragedy,
But when we love,
As described in Corinthians 13,
Our love will never fail,
And I will never regret it.

www.ingramcontent.com/pod-product-compliance
Lightning Source LLC
LaVergne TN
LVHW010827200726
843508LV00012B/2522